D0816423

Paul Erickson

THE PIER AT THE END OF THE WORLD

Photographs by Andrew Martinez

Tilbury House Publishers
Thomaston, Maine

Far from cities, bright lights, highways, and your neighborhood, an old wooden pier teeters and creaks at the edge of a cold sea. Once the pier was a busy place. Fishermen tied their boats alongside while they unloaded lobsters, herring, and cod.

But that was long ago. Today, the pier is crumbling into the sea. As dawn breaks at low tide, the pier's decaying skeleton stands out in the low light. Tall wooden poles, called pilings, hold up a few weather-beaten boards. Around the bases of the pilings, the sea gurgles.

Although people have abandoned the pier, other forms of life thrive beneath it. Thousands of strange and beautiful sea creatures prowl, crawl, slither, and swim through a mysterious undersea jungle of broken pilings and the pier's old stone foundation.

In the world above, the sun climbs higher. But down here, much of the sunlight is either reflected off the water's surface or absorbed by seawater and [illegible]. Life flourishes in this murky green realm.

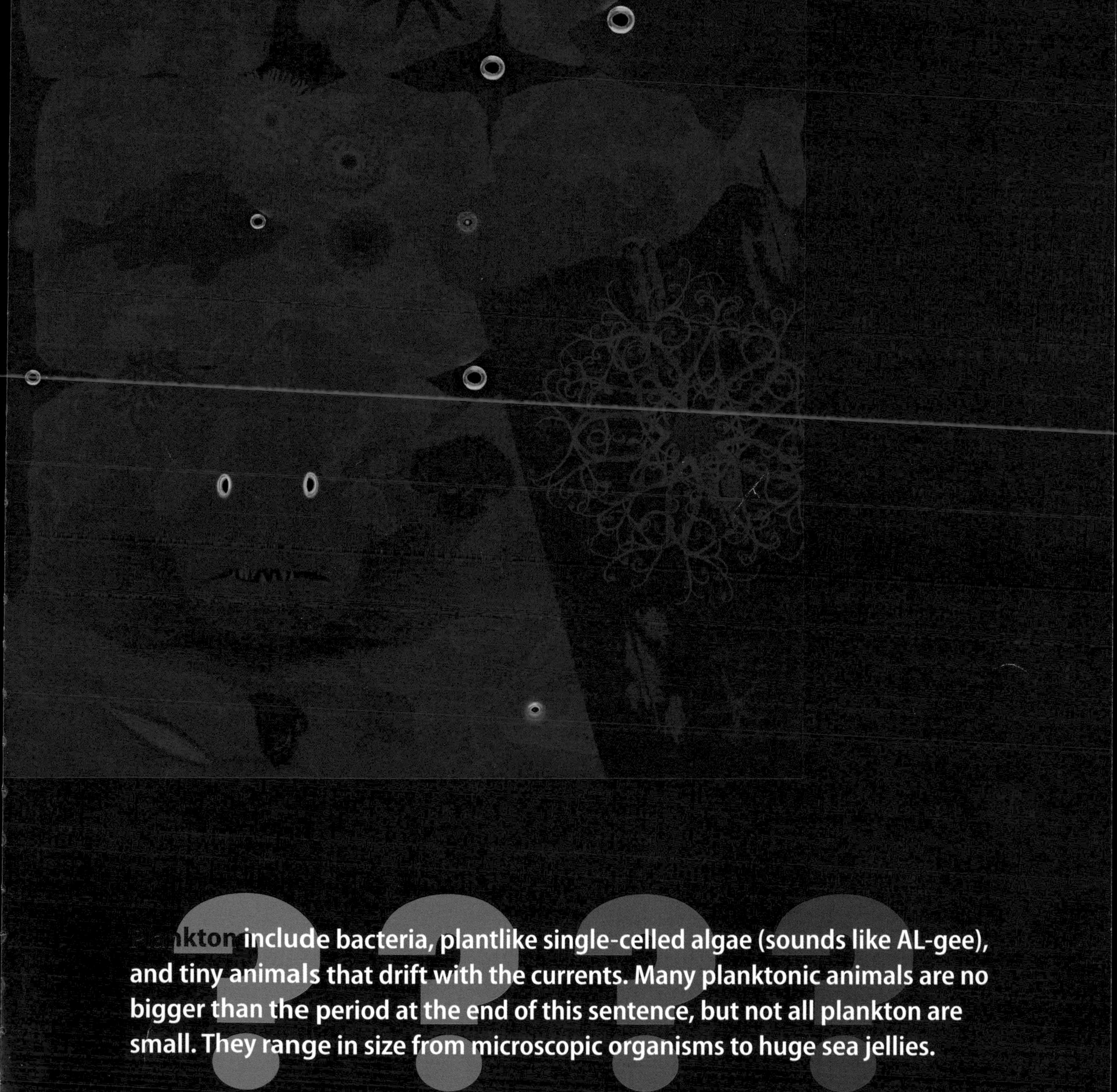

Plankton include bacteria, plantlike single-celled algae (sounds like AL-gee), and tiny animals that drift with the currents. Many planktonic animals are no bigger than the period at the end of this sentence, but not all plankton are small. They range in size from microscopic organisms to huge sea jellies.

If you could turn on bright lights and see clearly through the water, you would see a great variety of animals displaying brilliant colors, surprising shapes, and fantastic faces.

These animals have made it through another night in an undersea world full of hungry predators. Now that morning has arrived, they are venturing out from their nooks and crevices to find food and to survive—each in its own way.

Diversity means variety.
Biodiversity means variety of life.
Predators (sounds like PRED-uh-terz) are animals that feed on other animals. Apex predators are those at the top of the food chain.

Like a troll under a bridge, a **wolffish** lurks beneath the pier. This predator has just returned from a nighttime prowl. Using strong jaws with big teeth, it will crush and gulp down just about any living thing it can fit into its mouth. Although the wolffish may not be a picky eater, it is a prickly eater. It snacks on sea urchins—needle-sharp spines and all.

When New England fishermen haul wolffish into their boats, they take care not to let these four-foot-long monsters bite through their boots.

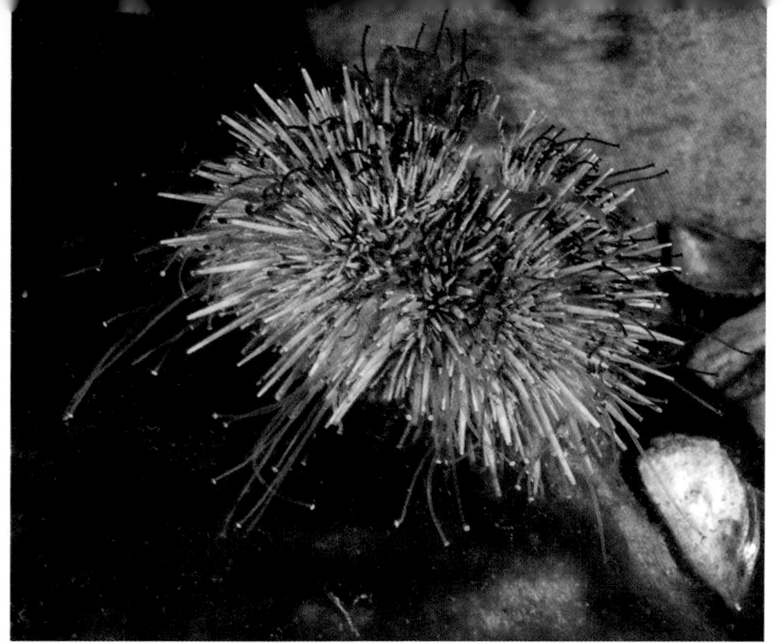

A sea urchin glides across surfaces on many tiny tube feet protruding from its body. Each foot is tipped with a suction cup that clings to surfaces.

A sea urchin can make itself look less like a bite-size snack for a wolffish by hiding under shells it picks up and attaches to itself using its tube feet.

Sea urchins are **echinoderms**, a group of animals that includes sea stars and sand dollars. Protecting the urchin are sharp spines and an **exoskeleton** shaped like a flattened globe. This living pincushion chews up and eats seaweed using five tiny teeth positioned around its circular mouth, which is centered on the underside of its body.

An **exoskeleton** (sounds like EX-oh-SKEL-uh-ton) is a hard, protective "outside skeleton" covering and protecting the soft interior of animals such as **echinoderms** (sounds like ee-KINE-oh-dermz) and crustaceans (krus-TAY-shunz)—a group that includes lobsters, crabs, and shrimp.

Sea anemones are beautiful but deadly to small animals.

Not far from the wolffish cave is a garden of animals called **sea anemones**, because they look like anemone flowers.

A relative of stinging sea jellies and corals, a sea anemone is little more than a fleshy column surrounding a big stomach. Atop the stomach is a mouth ringed with stinging tentacles that catch food and prevent other animals from nibbling on the anemone.

Anemones might look simple, but they are complex creatures. In each tentacle are intricate, microscopic, explosive stingers called **nematocysts**. When triggered by touch or certain chemicals, the stingers fire dart-like venomous threads into live food, including crabs, sea jellies, and fish. After the anemone stings, paralyzes, and captures a meal, the tentacles deliver it to the anemone's mouth.

A sea anemone devours an urchin, spines and all.

Some kinds of anemones from other parts of the world can sting people. But the northern red sea anemone shown here can't hurt you: Your skin is too thick.

Nematocysts sounds like nem-AT-oh-sists.

Northern red sea anemones are not always red.

Now it is noontime. The sun is high in the sky, and its rays penetrate the soupy water, illuminating bottom-dwelling fish beneath the pier.

The **spiny lumpsucker** looks like—well, a spiny lump. The skin on its belly can form a suction cup that lets the fish attach itself to rocks and other surfaces and stay in one place when strong tidal currents surge under the pier. Hanging on, barely moving a muscle, the lumpsucker snaps up shrimp and other small crustaceans that drift near its mouth.

A spiny lumpfish, showing the green glow of an eye.

Bulging lips make a fish called the **ocean pout** look unhappy—as if it is pouting. But that look is just an accident of nature. Its unusually wide mouth lets it gulp down scallops and other shellfish. The pout is well adapted for life in cold seawater: Its body contains chemicals that work like antifreeze.

Although the ocean pout has a long, slender body, this fish is not an eel. Instead, it is related to a family of mostly tropical ocean fish called blennies.

What other fish live on the bottom of the sea beneath the old pier?

Meet the **sea raven**. It has a big head with sharp spines. Even a wolffish would find this guy hard to swallow.

The sea raven's spines are superbly adapted defensive weapons.

While avoiding predators, a sea raven will swallow crabs, sea urchins, and other fish with its big mouth. Like many other bottom fish, a sea raven has no swim bladder—a balloon-like body part that prevents many kinds of fish from sinking to the bottom.

With skin colors and patterns matching the rocks and seaweeds around them, sea ravens and sculpins can hide in plain sight. Using their natural camouflage, they can sneak up on and attack other fish without being noticed. Small sea ravens and sculpins use their camouflage to hide from bigger fish, including other sea ravens and sculpins.

The sea raven camouflages itself with skin that looks like seaweed on its head.

Call him Mister Mom: This male **radiated shanny** guards a bunch of eggs that a female shanny left on the bottom. The devoted dad will guard the eggs all through the afternoon and the night that follows, and he will go on guarding them until they hatch.

Look closely. Can you spot fish eyes inside each egg?

The shanny is an important part of the ocean food chain: Millions of them are eaten by codfish—a popular, valuable seafood.

Hours pass. Afternoon sunlight angles across the sky now, shining on colorful sea creatures that live on the old pier's tumbledown foundation of granite blocks. Coating much of this stone wall is a crust of rock-hard pinkish algae. Among the animals clinging to the wall are many kinds of sea stars.

Like their cousins the sea urchins, **sea stars** move across surfaces on hundreds of tiny tube feet tipped with suction cups. And like sea urchins and sand dollars, sea stars have their mouths on the undersides of their bodies, right in the center.

A **winged sea star** with young stars growing under her skin. When the young are ready, they break out and crawl away.

Northern sea star, the common tidepool starfish

Horse star

Spiny sunstar

Sea stars have sloppy table manners. To eat a mussel or a clam, a sea star straddles its victim and attaches its arms and tube feet to each of the victim's two shells. Then the sea star tries to pull the shells apart. At first the shellfish is strong enough to resist, but eventually—sometimes hours later—its muscles get tired and its shells start to open. Even a slight opening is all the starfish needs to begin its meal. It then pushes its stomach out through its mouth and between the shells, and digests the internal soft body of the shellfish right where it sits.

Smooth sunstar

Badge star

What do you think this **polar sea star** is doing?

It is eating, using its many tube feet to open up a clam.

Here's another mollusk—one with shells. This is a **sea scallop**, and its two shells make it a **bivalved** mollusk like a clam or mussel. If you look carefully between the scallop's flattened shells, you'll see two rows of tiny eyes. Although these eyes can't see clear images, they can detect approaching ocean pout and other scallop-eating creatures.

The scallop usually sits in one place, but if danger comes near, it can swim up and away from the threat by quickly snapping its shells together. Every time the shells snap shut, a stream of water shoots out and thrusts the animal through the water. Imagine: a jet-propelled mollusk!

When no danger is present, the scallop waits for food to come to it. Like a grocery delivery service, powerful tidal currents carry microscopic plankton to the scallop. The scallop takes in the seawater and plankton. It filters the plankton from the water with tiny hairs on its gills, eats the plankton, and recycles the filtered water back into the sea. Clams and mussels do the same thing.

Bivalved sounds like BY-valved.

A sea scallop with shells partially open reveals two rows of tiny eyes.

Afternoon turns to evening, and the sun sinks below the horizon west of the pier at the end of the world, while the moon rises in the east. Shadows spread and deepen beneath the pier. Animals that are active during the day seek shelter and rest for the night. Others, though, are just leaving their daytime dens to go out and feed.

During daylight hours, this **redfish** hides behind the pier's old stone foundation, its large, light-sensitive eyes gazing out from cracks in the wall. At night, it swims from its shadowy crevices to eat small fish and shrimp. Its night vision is good, but it also uses other senses. Its keen sense of smell detects the odors of live food.

Although fish don't sleep like you do, they have slow-down times when they appear to be in a relaxed state, like someone in a daydream.

Perhaps you have seen blue crabs or rock crabs with their protective suits of armor. But their relative the **hermit crab**, with its soft fleshy tail, needs another way to protect itself. Its solution is to live in an empty shell. If a lobster or other predator approaches, the hermit crab can instantly curl up inside the shell. Then it blocks the shell's open end with its armored claws, much like shutting a door.

When a hermit crab outgrows its mobile home, it simply finds a slightly bigger shell. Then, in the blink of an eye, it moves its soft tail out of the old shell and into its new home.

At night, a hermit crab will go out for a walk to hunt for sea worms or perhaps a piece of rotting fish to nibble on. Yum!

With night coming on, a hermit crab without a shell is very vulnerable. This one finds temporary protection inside the exoskeleton of a dead sea urchin.

The lion has been called the King of Beasts, but the king under the old pier is a giant **American lobster** with claws bigger than baseball gloves. Weighing 35 pounds or more, this huge crustacean lives in a cave within the pier's stone wall. Most likely it's at least 50 years old.

Sometimes a lobster will use its claws to fight with other lobsters. And it can hold both claws together like the front end of a bulldozer to clear sand and pebbles from its burrow.

At night, lobsters often emerge from their burrows to find food. They hunt for fish, mussels, snails, other lobsters, and an occasional seaweed salad.

The American lobster has two kinds of front claws. It uses its fat crusher claw to break open shellfish and the thinner ripper claw to cut up its food.

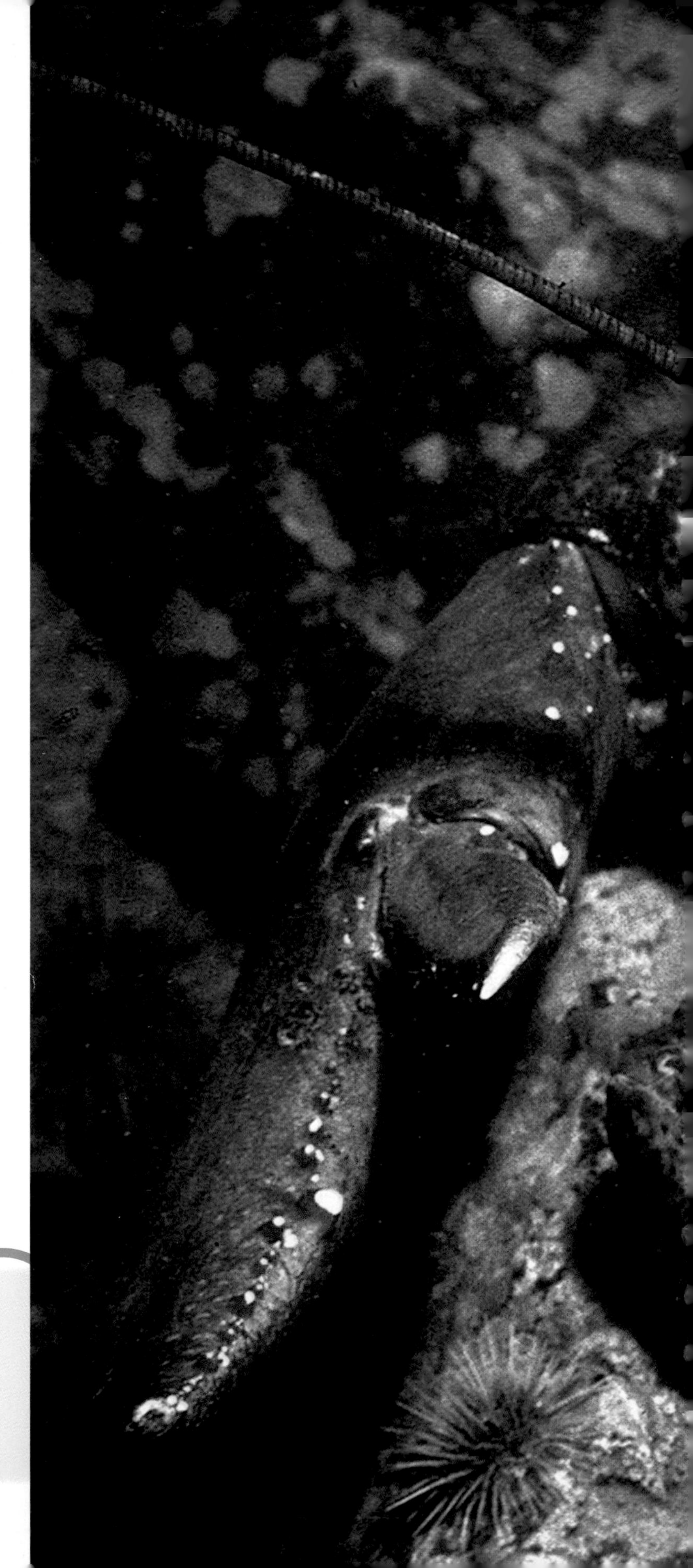

Paul Erickson photo

Now it is midnight under the pier. The night passes slowly in this cold, dark place. Predators roam, while the animals they're hunting for hunker in burrows, between rocks, or in any shelter they can find.

Another sunrise lights up the pier at the end of the world.
The lobsters, redfish, and other night predators have gone back to their daytime shelters.

Most creatures under the pier stay close to the shelters they know.
They don't stray far unless forced by hunger or pursuing predators.

Let's compare this picture with the one on pages 6 and 7.
Which animals have been eaten or moved away?
Which animals have changed their locations?

1. The hermit crab and spiny lumpsucker swapped positions.
2. The kelp drifts upward in the current.
3. The sea slug has moved around the bolt.
4. The lower groups of mussels are gone, perhaps eaten by wolffish.
5. The sea scallop swam away or was eaten.
6. The urchin on the middle piling has moved up.
7. The nearest urchin is gone (note shells under wolffish).
8. On the far left piling, the sunstars swapped positions.
9. The middle redfish now faces right.
10. The largest redfish moved down behind the piling on the right.
11. A light-colored redfish at the top moved left.
12. Many redfish (eyes) behind the wall have moved.
13. The top left redfish moved down the wall.
14. The top sunstar moved to the right.
15. The giant lobster is behind the pilings at left.

Little Wonders

Many of the animals living under the pier are small and easy to overlook. But they are just as important to the balance of nature as their larger neighbors. You've already met some of them. Here are some more:

Unlike stony reef-building corals, **sea strawberry soft coral** does not form a sturdy skeleton around itself. Instead, this colony of animals is soft and flexible. Sometimes, soft coral contracts into a lump. Then, when ocean currents flow, it fills with seawater and blossoms into the shape of a miniature branching tree. Once inflated, it catches and eats plankton using its tiny tentacles.

Although this little animal may look like a clam, the **northern lamp shell** is not closely related to clams and other mollusks. Instead, it is a **brachiopod**. Hundreds of millions of years ago, more than 30,000 kinds of brachiopods lived in the sea. Most of them became extinct, and today only about 380 living species have been identified.

Brachiopod sounds like BRAK-ee-oh-pod. The shape of the northern lamp shell resembles an ancient Roman oil lamp.

The **anemone sea spider** belongs to a group of animals called **pycnogonids**. As you may have guessed, these sea creatures remind people of land spiders, which are air-breathing **arachnids**. Using a tube on its head, the sea spider sucks juices from sea anemones. It's like drinking from a juice box using a straw.

Pycnogonids sounds like pic-no-GON-idz.
Arachnids sounds like ahr-AK-nidz.

The **slime fan worm** slips its body into tiny crevices and fans out a soft, plankton-catching structure around its exposed mouth. If an animal comes near, the worm instantly pulls the fan back inside its body. Triggering this vanishing act is a giant nerve running the length of the worm. The big, relatively easy-to-study nerve has helped scientists learn how animal nervous systems work.

Belonging to a group of animals called sea squirts, or **tunicates**, the **sea vase** creates a current of seawater in and out of its body. As it does so, it catches and eats tiny particles of food within the current. A newly hatched tunicate larva looks like a tiny tadpole. After a while, the larva attaches to a surface and grows into a permanently anchored sea squirt.

Tunicate sounds like TUNE-uh-kit.

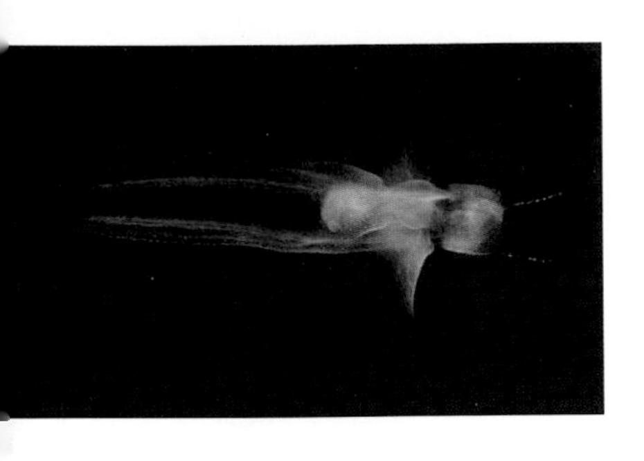

The **naked sea butterfly**, also called a sea angel, is a pteropod, a planktonic mollusk. Its adult stage has no shell. It uses its side fins to swim and hover in the water column as currents carry it. When naked sea butterflies gather by the thousands, whales will feast on them.

Young **Aesop shrimp** display distinctive red stripes across their see-through shells. This shrimp eats tiny crustaceans and hydroids. Typically walking on the bottom of the sea all day long, Aesop shrimp rise (migrate) vertically into the water column at night. The Aesop shrimp lives as far north as the Arctic Ocean.

Aesop sounds like A-sop.

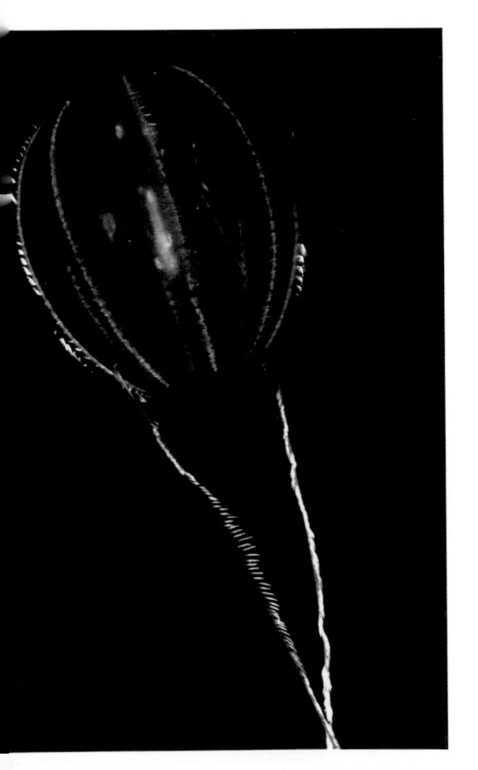

This **sea gooseberry** belongs to a group of gelatinous ocean animals called **ctenophores**. Unlike many sea jellies, ctenophores have no stingers. The sea gooseberry drifts with ocean currents, catching microscopic sea life in its tentacles. It can also propel itself a little by moving tiny hairlike structures called **cilia**.

Ctenophore sounds like TEN-uh-for (the first letter, "c," is silent).
Cilia sounds like SIL-ee-uh

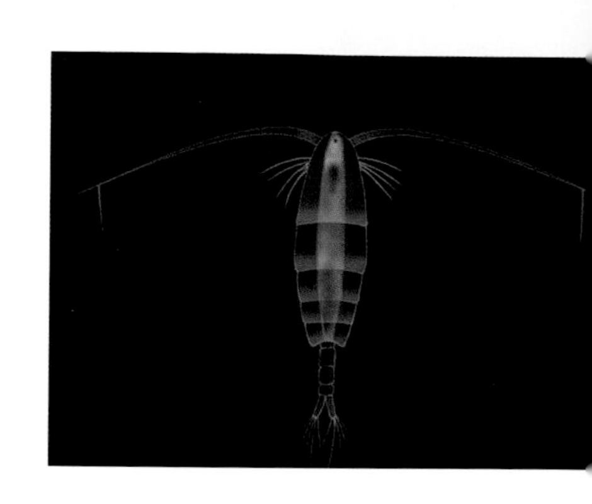

Copepods, many of which are planktonic, are related to crabs, lobsters, and other crustaceans. Unlike fish, copepods have no gills. Instead, they absorb oxygen directly from seawater. Important players in the ocean food web, copepods are "primary consumers," feeding on diatoms and other kinds of **phytoplankton**. In the sea, copepods are devoured by animals as small as a shrimp and as large as a whale.

Copepod sounds like COPE-uh-pod.
Phytoplankton are microscopic plantlike algae that drift with water currents.

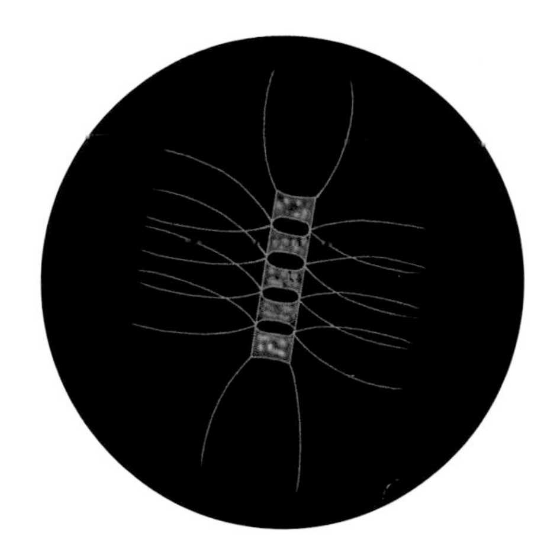

Like other kinds of phytoplankton (and like most land plants too), **diatoms** use solar energy to turn water and carbon dioxide into oxygen and food in the process called photosynthesis. In turn, diatoms are gobbled up by copepods and other kinds of animal plankton. As "primary producers," diatoms play a major role at the base of the ocean food chain.

Diatom sounds like DYE-uh-tom.
Photosynthesis sounds like fo-toe-SYN-thuh-sis.

Species in order of appearance

1. **Wolffish**
Anarhichas lupus
Length: up to 4 feet (1.2 m)
Diet: sea urchins, mussels, other invertebrates, and small fish

2. **Green Sea Urchin**

Strongylocentrotus droebachiensis
Diameter: up to 3 inches (8 cm)
Diet: algae (seaweeds)

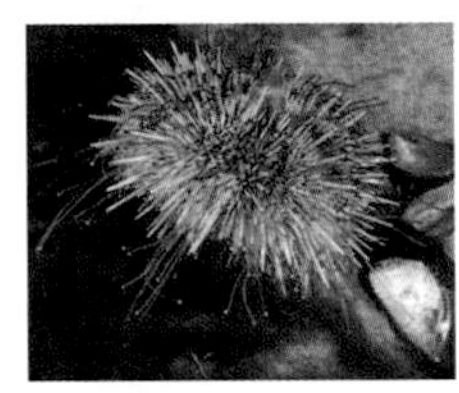

3. **Northern Red Sea Anemone**
Urticina felina
Height: up to 5 inches (13 cm)
Diet: crabs, shrimp, sea jellies, sea urchins, and small fish

4. **Atlantic Spiny Lumpsucker**
Eumicrotremus spinosus
Length: up to 3 inches (8 cm)
Diet: comb jellies and other sea jellies, and shrimp

5. **Ocean Pout**
Zoarces americanus
Length: up to 3 feet (91 cm)
Diet: mussels, crabs, whelks, sea scallops, sea urchins, and sand dollars

6. **Sea Raven**
Hemitripterus americanus
Length: up to 20 inches (51 cm)
Diet: crabs, sea urchins, other invertebrates, and small fish

7. **Radiated Shanny**
Ulvaria subbifurcata
Length: up to 6 inches (15 cm)
Diet: worms and crustaceans

8. **Sea Stars**

Northern Sea Star
Asterias rubens

Horse Star
Hippasteria phrygiana

Winged Sea Star
Pteraster militaris

Spiny Sunstar
Crossaster papposus

Smooth Sunstar
Solaster endeca

Badge Star
Porania insignis

Polar Sea Star
Leptasterias polaris

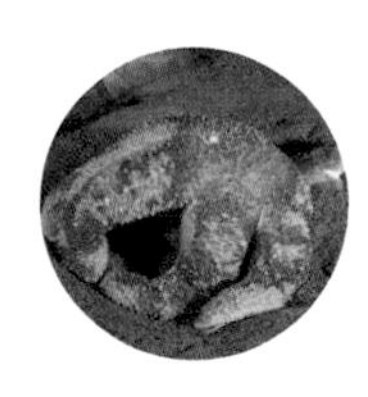

Diameter: from 6 inches (16 cm) for winged sea star and badge star to 16 inches (40 cm) for northern sea star, horse star, and smooth sunstar
Diet: invertebrates, sponges (winged sea star), and detritus (badge star)

9. **Northern Basket Star**
Gorgonocephalus arcticus
Diameter: up to 28 inches (72 cm)
Diet: zooplankton

10. **Red-finger Aeolis Sea Slug**
(Nudibranch)
Flabellina verrucosa

Length: up to 1.25 inches (3 cm)

Diet*:* hydroids

11. **Sea Scallop**
Placopecten magellanicus

Diameter: up to 6 inches (15 cm)

Diet: diatoms and other kinds of phytoplankton

12. **Acadian Redfish**
Sebastes fasciatus

Length: up to 16 inches (41 cm)
Diet: shrimp, small fish, and copepods

13. **Acadian Hermit Crab**
Pagurus acadianus

Length: up to 1.25 inches (3 cm)

Diet: omnivorous, including seaweeds (algae) and decaying sea life

14. **American Lobster**
Homarus americanus

Length: up to 24 inches (61 cm), record sizes up to 3.25 feet (1 m) and more than 40 pounds (18 kg)

Diet: sea urchins, many other invertebrates, seaweeds, and decaying sea life

15. **Sea Strawberry Soft Coral**
Gersemia rubiformis

Height: up to 4 inches (10 cm)

Diet: diatoms and other kinds of phytoplankton

16. **Northern Lamp Shell**
Terebratulina septentrionalis

Length: up to 1 inch (2.5 cm)

Diet: diatoms and other kinds of phytoplankton, and decaying food particles

17. **Anemone Sea Spider**
Pycnogonum littorale

Width: up to a half inch (1.3 cm)

Diet: internal fluids of sea anemones

18. **Slime Fan Worm**
Myxicola infundibulum

Length: up to 8 inches (20 cm)

Diet: diatoms, other kinds of plankton, and decaying food particles

19. **Sea Vase**
Ciona intestinalis

Size: up to 4 inches (10 cm)

Diet: plankton and organic detritus

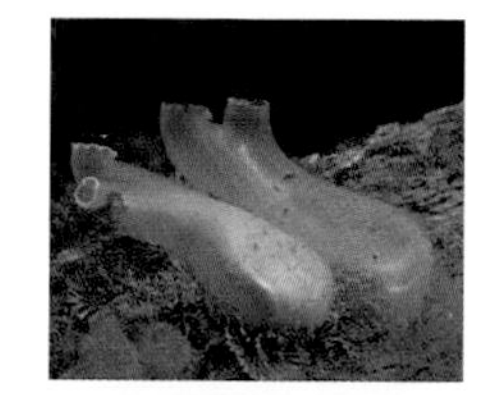

20. **Naked Sea Butterfly** (pteropod)
Clione limacine

Length: up to 1.5 inches (3.8 cm)

Diet: swimming sea snails

21. **Aesop Shrimp**
Pandalus montagui

Length: up to 4 inches (10 cm)

Diet: copepods and hydroids

22. **Sea Gooseberry**
Pleurobrachia pileus

Diameter: up to 1 inch (2.5 cm)

Diet: copepods and fish larvae

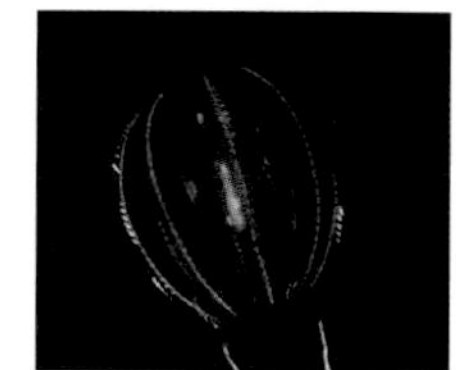

23. **Copepod**
Calanus finmarchicus

Length: up to one-sixth of an inch (4 mm)

Diet: diatoms

24. **Diatom**
Chaetoceros spp.

Size: microscopic

Diet: produces and stores its own food (autotrophic)

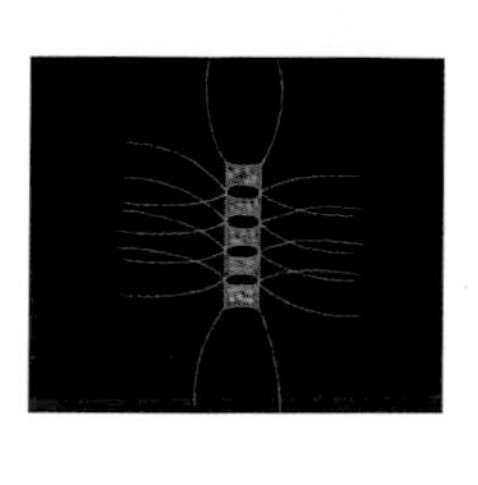

Tilbury House Publishers
12 Starr Street
Thomaston, Maine 04861
800-582-1899
www.tilburyhouse.com

To Carl and Doris Erickson, who brought me to the sea.—PE

To the memory of my father, Andres, and those countless days with him at the piers in Boston Harbor on the towboat Hercules.—AM

First hardcover edition: October 2014 • 10 9 8 7 6 5 4 3 2 1

ISBN 978-0-88448-382-3

Library of Congress Cataloging-in-Publication Data

Erickson, Paul, 1952– The pier at the end of the world / Paul Erickson; with photographs by Andrew Martinez. pages cm ISBN 978-0-88448-382-3 1. Marine animals—Juvenile literature. I. Martinez, Andrew J., 1946– photographer. II. Title. QL122.2.E753 2014 591.77—dc23 2014027249

Cover design by Ann Casady. Interior design by Kathy Squires.

Printed by Worzalla, Stevens Point, WI.

Scan the code to visit the Tilbury Learning Center.

Author's note: The pier at the end of the world is in the Gulf of Maine. We can't reveal its exact location because the rich habitat could be harmed by collectors.